Pan American Book Co.
Bilingual · Bicultural School Supplies
4362 Melrose Av., L.A., 29, Ca. · 665-1241

The Adventures of Connie and Diego

Las aventuras de Connie y Diego

Written by / Escrito por Maria Garcia
Illustrated by / Ilustrado por Malaquias Montoya
Translated into Spanish by / Traducido al español por Alma Flor Ada

Children's Book Press / Libros para niños

Once upon a time,
Connie and Diego were born
in the Land of Plenty.

Hace mucho tiempo
nacieron Connie y Diego
en la Tierra de la Abundancia.

2

Their sisters and brothers
all gathered around the crib
to look at the twins.
But when they saw the babies,
were they ever surprised.
Connie and Diego were
different from the other children.

Todos sus hermanas y hermanos se
reunieron alrededor de la cuna
para ver a los gemelos.
Pero cuando los vieron
se sorprendieron muchísimo:
Connie y Diego eran muy
diferentes de cualquier otro niño.

4

The twins were born with many
colors all over their little bodies.
They looked so funny
that their sisters and brothers
started to laugh.
They laughed and they laughed,
and from that day on,
everyone laughed
at Connie and Diego.

Los cuerpecitos de los gemelos
eran de muchos colores.
Se veían tan cómicos
que sus hermanas y hermanos
se echaron a reir.
Se rieron y rieron
y a partir de ese día
todo el mundo se río
de Connie y de Diego.

Poor Connie and Diego!
One day they got tired
of being laughed at,
and they decided to run away.

"Maybe we will find a place
where no one will make
fun of us," Diego said,
as they dried
each other's tears.

So they ran and they ran
until they reached a forest
where they made a bed
of leaves under a tree
and went to sleep.

¡Pobres Connie y Diego!
Un día se cansaron
de que se rieran de ellos
y decidieron escaparse.

—Quizás encontremos un lugar
donde nadie se burle
de nosotros— dijo Diego.
Y cariñosamente se secaron
las lágrimas el uno al otro.

Y corrieron y corrieron
hasta que llegaron a un bosque
donde se hicieron una cama
de hojas bajo un árbol
y se acostaron a dormir.

The next morning
they were startled
by a big brown bear.
"Could we live here with you?"
they asked, after
telling him their story.

"No, you can't,"
growled the bear.
"You have no fur
to keep you warm.
You couldn't survive
in the cold, cold woods."
And he sent them sadly
on their way.

A la mañana siguiente
los sorprendió
un enorme oso pardo.
— ¿Podemos vivir aquí contigo?—
Le preguntaron después
de contarle su historia.

— No, de ninguna manera—
gruñó el oso.
—Ustedes no tienen una piel peluda
que los mantenga abrigados.
No podrían sobrevivir
en los fríos bosques.
Y les ordenó
irse.

Pretty soon they came
to an ocean.
As they were wondering
how to get across,
they saw a huge whale
spouting steam
as she rose out of the water.
They told her their story,
and then they asked,
"Can we live here with you?"

"I'm sorry but you can't,"
she answered.
"We whales live most of
our lives under water
and only come up for air.
But if you wish,
I could help you get
to the other side."

Muy pronto llegaron
a un océano.
Mientras se preguntaban
como harían para cruzar
vieron una inmensa ballena
lanzando su chorro de vapor
al asomarse a la superficie.
Le contaron su historia
y luego le preguntaron:
—¿Podemos vivir contigo?

—Lo siento, pero no es posible—
contestó la ballena.
—Vivimos la mayor parte
de nuestras vidas bajo el agua
y solamente salimos a respirar.
Pero si lo desean
los puedo ayudar a llegar
al otro lado.

So the twins built
a wooden raft.
As they were being
pushed across the ocean
by the whale,
they saw a beautiful eagle
flying overhead.

"What wonderful colors you have!"
screeched the bird.
"Come fly with me!"
And away it flew,
disappearing into the clouds.

Entonces los gemelos construyeron
una balsa de madera.
Mientras la ballena
los empujaba a través
del océano
vieron una hermosa águila
volando sobre ellos.

—¡Qué magníficos colores tienen!—
chilló el ave.
—¡Vengan a volar conmigo!
Y desapareció
volando entre las nubes.

"Wait for us!"
cried Connie and Diego
as they flapped
their arms furiously.
But of course,
they couldn't fly.

—¡Espéranos!—
Gritaron Connie y Diego
y agitaron
sus bracitos furiosamente.
Pero, por supuesto,
no pudieron volar.

14

When the twins reached
the other side
of the ocean,
they found themselves
in a deep, dark jungle.
Suddenly,
they heard an angry roar.

"What are you doing here?"
demanded a big
ferocious-looking tiger.

Cuando los gemelos llegaron
al otro lado
del océano
se encontraron
en una profunda selva obscura.
De repente
oyeron un fiero rugido.

—¿Qué hacen ustedes aquí?—
les interrogó un tigre grande
de apariencia muy feroz.

16

At first, the twins were afraid
of being eaten,
so they quickly
told their story.
Then they added timidly,
"We've wandered so far and so long
and we still haven't found
where we belong.
Couldn't we live here with you?"

"No, you cannot!"
roared the tiger.
"Tigers and humans
do not get along together.
Humans hunt and kill us.
They build roads and houses
on our home."

Al principio los gemelos tenían miedo
de que el tigre se los comiera,
así que contaron su historia
rápidamente.
Luego añadieron tímidamente:
—Hemos andado tanto y tanto
y todavía no hemos encontrado
el lugar que nos corresponde.
¿No podríamos vivar aquí contigo?

—¡No, de ninguna manera!—
rugió el tigre.
—Los tigres y los humanos
no se llevan bien.
Los humanos nos cazan y nos matan.
Construyen caminos y casas
en nuestros hogares.

Connie and Diego began to cry.
Hand in hand
they sadly walked away.

"Oh, come back!" snarled the tiger.
"Stop crying and look at yourselves!
Look at your hands.
Aren't they for building?
Look at your legs.
Aren't they for walking?"

"But look at us.
We're all different colors,"
sobbed the twins.

Connie y Diego empezaron a llorar.
Cogidos de la mano
se fueron caminando tristemente.

—¡Vengan acá!— les gritó el tigre.
—¡Dejen de llorar y mírense un momento!
Mírense las manos.
¿No están hechas para construir?
Mírense las piernas. ¿No están
hechas para caminar?

—Pero míranos.
Somos de todos los colores—
sollozaron los gemelos.

"Bah, that's not important!"
snapped the tiger.
"You're human! Can't you see?"

The twins looked
at each other and
for the first time
they were not troubled by
their many colors.

—¡Que va, eso no tiene importancia!—
replicó el tigre.
—¡Ustedes son humanos! ¿No lo ven?

Los gemelos se miraron
el uno al otro y
por primera vez
ya no les molestaron
sus muchos colores.

"We're human,"
echoed Connie, "just like
our sisters and brothers."

Then Connie took Diego's hand
and gently said,
"Let's go home."

—Somos humanos—
repitió Connie —igual que
nuestras hermanas y nuestros hermanos.

Y Connie cogió a Diego de la mano
y le dijo cariñosamente:
—Vámonos a casa.

So Connie and Diego went home
where nothing had changed.
But they had changed,
because now they knew
that they belonged with
their sisters and brothers.

Y Connie y Diego regresaron a su casa
donde nada había cambiado.
Pero ellos habían cambiado
porque ahora sabían
que allí, con sus hermanas
y hermanos, estaba su lugar.

And from that day on,
the story of Connie and Diego
was told throughout
the Land of Plenty.

Y desde ese día
la historia de Connie y de Diego
se ha contado a través
de la Tierra de la Abundancia.

23

The Author Talks about her Story

When I first started writing this little story it was very difficult for me. I had never done anything like this before, and I didn't know how to begin. I have seven children living with me — six of my own and one who is my cousin — and so I asked them to tell me stories. Then I read several children's books and a book of fables. What finally began to emerge from my thoughts was a need to write about who I am and what I believe in.

When I was a young girl, my mother used to tell me stories about my great-grandmother, who is still alive. They were stories of poverty, endurance and dignity. Great-grandma is a very proud woman and her life has been an example of "¡Jalisco no se raja!" ("She never gives up!") Her parents were Kiowa, Yaqui, Spanish and French. And this is who I am. I am Chicana. I am Black. I am Native American. I am Asian. I am White. What does this mean? To children it can be very confusing. I hope this little story conveys my feelings that we are all human beings and we should be proud of who we are.

¡Unidos hasta la victoria! ¡Venceremos!
— Maria Garcia

Author Maria Garcia was born in Kennedy, Texas, in 1944. When she wrote this story she lived in San Jose, California, and worked in Oakland for the Comité de México y Aztlán (COMEXAZ), an educational research service which gathered news about Chicanos and Mexicanos in California and the Southwest.

Artist Malaquias Montoya was born in Albuquerque, New Mexico, in 1938. As a child he remembers following the fruit harvest in California's San Joaquin Valley and learning to draw on the paper trays which were used to hold the grapes while they were drying. "Not having anything to play with," he says, "we used the creativity we were all born with."

Editor: Harriet Rohmer
Design of the original edition: Harriet Rohmer, Robin Cherin, Roger I Reyes. Design of this edition: Mira Reisberg.
Production of the original edition: Robin Cherin. Production of this edition: Tony Yuen.

Library of Congress Cataloging-in-Publication Data
García, Maria, 1944- The adventures of Connie and Diego= Las aventuras de Connie y Diego.
(Fifth world tales=Cuentos del quinto mundo) English and Spanish.
Summary: Tired of being laughed at because they are different, a pair of multicolored twins run away to ask the animals where they really belong.
1. Spanish language-Readers. [1. Prejudices - Fiction. 2. Twins - Fiction. 3. Brothers and sisters - Fiction. 4. Spanish language materials - Bilingual.]
I. Montoya, Malaquias, 1938 - ill. II. Title: Aventuras de Connie y Diego. IV. Series: Fifth world tales.
PC4115.G333 1986   468.6'421 [Fic]   86-17132   ISBN: 0-89239-028-X